T0131638

AVA BAVA PRESENTS

An Affirmations Journal

NASTASSJA PATMON

authorHOUSE

AuthorHouse™
1663 Liberty Drive
Bloomington, IN 47403
www.authorhouse.com
Phone: 1 (800) 839-8640

Published by AuthorHouse 03/18/2020

ISBN: 978-1-7283-5182-7 (sc)
ISBN: 978-1-7283-5180-3 (hc)
ISBN: 978-1-7283-5181-0 (e)

Library of Congress Control Number: 2020905304

Dear _____

This journal was created for you to help reinforce
the reasons why you are a gift to
your family, your friends,
and the world!

Jot down cool ideas, the fun day you had,
or how you are feeling.
When you look back,
you'll see how much you have grown
and how far you have come.

Remember! It's okay to be shy. It's okay to be funny.
It's okay to laugh and it's okay
to feel bad sometimes.
Just make sure you never forget, it's
okay to be exactly who you are
Because you are a gift.

K, bye! Auntie Nik :)

I am _____

I am _____

I am _____

I am _____

I am _____

Words are powerful! What you believe about yourself is how you will carry yourself.

Who do you believe you are? What qualities do you like about yourself? What interests you? What makes you happy? The answers to these questions will help you to understand what is important to you.

You will also discover that by the end of this journal, your answers might change. That's okay! It's called growth. You are going to evolve into the adult you are supposed to be, but it all starts with how you see yourself today.

I have so much to offer

What's an affirmation?
An affirmation is a statement that
you are confident about.

What's a positive affirmation?
A positive comment or thought that
encourages you or someone else.

It is your job to make sure you have a great
day. Positive affirmations are to comfort you
when you're feeling low, encourage you when
you're feeling unsure, and strength you when
you are feeling like vou are not enough.
♡

Let's practice!
Now that you know what an affirmation is,
think of five new words to describe yourself.

I am _____
I am _____
I am _____
I am _____
I am _____

♡

Hey girl, hey!

Today's Date _____

Today was a good day because…

_____

_____

_____

_____

_____

_____

_____

Today could have been better if…

_____

_____

_____

_____

_____

_____

_____

But I am still grateful for…

_____

_____

_____

_____

_____

_____

_____

The best is yet to come!

Today's Date _____

Random thoughts...

_____

_____

_____

_____

_____

_____

_____

_____

Random thoughts...

♡

I love being me, there's no one else I'd rather be!

Today's Date _____

Random thoughts…

_____

_____

_____

_____

_____

_____

_____

_____

_____

_____

_____

_____

_____

Today's Date _____

Random thoughts…

_____

_____

_____

_____

_____

_____

_____

_____

_____

_____

_____

_____

_____

_____

_____

♡

I'm perfectly imperfect and that's cool with me!

Today's Date _____

Random thoughts...

_____

_____

_____

_____

_____

_____

_____

_____

_____

_____

_____

_____

_____

_____

_____

Today's Date _____

Random thoughts...

_____

_____

_____

_____

_____

_____

_____

_____

_____

_____

_____

_____

_____

_____

_____

_____

_____

I'm legit!

Today's Date _____

Random thoughts…

_____

_____

_____

_____

_____

_____

_____

_____

_____

_____

_____

_____

_____

_____

Today's Date _____

Random thoughts...

_____

_____

_____

_____

_____

_____

_____

_____

_____

_____

_____

_____

_____

_____

_____

_____

_____

♡

I'm dope, in real life!

Today's Date _____

Random thoughts...

_____

_____

_____

_____

_____

_____

_____

_____

_____

_____

_____

_____

_____

Random thoughts...

_____

_____

_____

_____

_____

_____

_____

_____

_____

_____

_____

_____

_____

_____

_____

♡

I don't want to be them; I'd rather be me.

Have you noticed that you are different from your friends? That's a good thing!

Reasons being different is a GIFT!

- You will offer a different opinion to a conversation
- You can learn from your friend
- They can learn from you
- You will stand out
- You don't have to pretend to be anyone else

What are some other reasons why being different is dope?

- _____
- _____
- _____
- _____
- _____
- _____

You can't spell FUN without 'U'!

I am tall
I am Black
I am funny
I am caring
I am a sister
I am an athlete
I am a vibe
Kamara, age 13

I am beautiful
I am strong
I am smart
I am talented
I am faithful
I am healthy
I am Sasha Fierce
Mya, age 14

You can't spell TEAM without ME!

I am smart
I am funny
I am kind
I am a best friend
I am a daughter
I am a singer
I am a dancer
Kayden, age 10

I am unsure
I am shy
I am reserved
I am kind of smart
I am weird
I am loyal
I am aware
Kyra, age 14

You're the bomb. Com!

I am kind
I am beautiful
I am smart
I am short-ish
I am cool
I am fun
I am the favorite
Natalia, age 13

I am beautiful
I am a child of God
I am happy
I am loving
I am nice
I am kind
I am Nigerian
Ciara, age 13

♡

I know my potential!

You will notice that your friends may have attributes that you do not possess. Compliment them! But remember just because you don't have that same attribute doesn't take away from what you have to offer. You have something they don't have and that's your superpower.

What are some things you love about your friends?

_____

_____

_____

_____

_____

_____

_____

_____

_____

_____

When you appreciate your friends, it shows that you accept them for who they are. The same way you appreciate your friends should be the same way you appreciate yourself too. Flaws and all!

I don't compete with my friends, I congratulate them!

Today's Date _____

Random thoughts…

_____

_____

_____

_____

_____

_____

_____

_____

_____

_____

_____

_____

_____

_____

_____

_____

Today's Date _____

Random thoughts...

_____

_____

_____

_____

_____

_____

_____

_____

_____

_____

_____

_____

_____

_____

Self-Love is the best love

Today's Date _____

Random thoughts...

_____

_____

_____

_____

_____

_____

_____

_____

_____

_____

_____

_____

_____

_____

_____

_____

Random thoughts...

_____

_____

_____

_____

_____

_____

_____

_____

_____

_____

_____

_____

_____

_____

_____

♡

I don't live by their standards of me.

Random thoughts...

Today's Date _____

Random thoughts...

_____

_____

_____

_____

_____

_____

_____

_____

_____

_____

_____

_____

_____

Watch me work!

Today's Date _____

Random thoughts…

_____

_____

_____

_____

_____

_____

_____

_____

_____

_____

_____

_____

_____

_____

_____

Random thoughts...

_____

_____

_____

_____

_____

_____

_____

_____

_____

_____

_____

_____

_____

♡

I'm capable of a lot!

Today's Date _____

Random thoughts…

_____

_____

_____

_____

_____

_____

_____

_____

_____

_____

_____

_____

_____

_____

Random thoughts...

_____

_____

_____

_____

_____

_____

_____

_____

_____

_____

_____

_____

_____

♡

I am unapologetically me!

Do you know what you want to be when you grow up? Do you have multiple talents? Which one is your favorite? You don't have to limit yourself to one thing, but if there is something important to you, you should practice it to become great at it.

My favorite thing to do is...

_____

_____

_____

_____

My second favorite thing to do is...

_____

_____

_____

_____

My third favorite thing to do is...

_____

_____

_____

_____

What does it mean to be a follower?

*A person who moves or travels behind
someone or something.*

*Don't be a follower! You are not going to like everything
your friends do and that is okay! Don't do things
that will make you uncomfortable just to please other
people. It's okay to say, "Nah". It's okay to say, "I will
see you guys next time".*

Why do you think it's important to be an individual?

- _____
- _____
- _____
- _____
- _____

*When you think for yourself that means you do not
allow others to make decisions for you. Even when you
agree with them, it's because you have decided to, not
because they told you to. When you practice thinking
for yourself, you are building your confidence and
personality. Your thoughts and opinions are important.
Do not give the power of thinking for yourself, away!*

Be you! Everyone else is taken.

Today was a good day because...

_____

_____

_____

_____

_____

_____

_____

_____

Today could have been better if...

_____

_____

_____

_____

_____

_____

_____

_____

But I am still grateful for…

_____

_____

_____

_____

_____

_____

_____

_____

The best is yet to come!

I hope you have enjoyed these affirmation exercises. It is my desire that you continue to learn about yourself and grow into a strong, confident, and happy young lady.
If you are all those things already, good! Keep shining! Obstacles will come and disappointments will happen, but do not lose sight of who you are. You are loved. You are necessary. You are a gift. Continue to use this journal to express yourself, create, or however you see fit. Whatever you do, just don't stop being a gift to yourself and to others.

...

Printed in the United States
By Bookmasters